FIRST CODING

LOGIC

By Sam Thompson

Gareth Stevens
PUBLISHING

Please visit our website, www.garethstevens.com. For a free color catalog of all our high-quality books, call toll free 1-800-542-2595 or fax 1-877-542-2596.

Cataloging-in-Publication Data
Names: Thompson, Sam.
Title: Logic / Sam Thompson.
Description: New York : Gareth Stevens, 2022. | Series: First coding | Includes glossary and index.
Identifiers: ISBN 9781538274439 (pbk.) | ISBN 9781538274453 (library bound) | ISBN 9781538274446 (6 pack) | ISBN 9781538274460 (ebook)
Subjects: LCSH: Computer logic–Juvenile literature.
Classification: LCC QA76.9.L63 T466 2022 | DDC 005.101'5113–dc23

This edition is published by arrangement with Booklife Publishing

Published in 2022 by
Gareth Stevens Publishing
29 E. 21st Street
New York, NY 10010

Written by: Sam Thompson
Edited by: Madeline Tyler
Designed by: Dan Scase

Printed in the United States of America

CPSIA compliance information: Batch #CWGS22: For further information contact Gareth Stevens, New York, New York at 1-800-542-2595.

Photo credits

All images are courtesy of Shutterstock.com. With thanks to Getty Images, Thinkstock Photo and iStockphoto. Front page - RoryDesign, the_same_space, Lineicons freebird, Happy Art, RaulAlmu, airdone, paulaphoto. 4&5 - wavebreakmedia. 6&7 - AlesiaKan, NuPenDekDee, Jane Kelly. 8&9 - Chatchawan. 10&11 - ProStockStudio. 12&13 - BEST-BACKGROUNDS, Yuriy Golub. 14&15 - Paolo De Gasperis, TippaPatt. 16&17 - Sira Anamwong. 18&19 - Hung Chung Chih. 20&21 - Andrey_Popov. 22&23 - ©daisuke1230. Background on all pages - magic pictures. Tablet - Olga Lebedeva. Icons - RoryDesign, the_same_space, Lineicons freebird, Happy Art, RaulAlmu. Background on all pages – magic pictures. Tablet – Olga Lebedeva. Icons – RoryDesign, the_same_space, Lineicons freebird, Happy Art, RaulAlmu.

CONTENTS

Words that look like <u>this</u> can be found in the glossary on page 24.

WHAT IS CODING?

Coding means telling a computer what to do by writing a set of instructions. The set of instructions is called a code. We use coding to do all sorts of amazing things on a computer.

Another name for coding is programming.

A computer is a machine that can follow instructions and store information.

Information is the numbers and facts that tell you about something.

Someone who writes code is called a programmer.

Bits of information are put together to make a program. The program is then run on a computer.

WHAT IS LOGIC?

A piece of code is full of choices that a computer has to make. Logic is the way that a computer chooses what to do.

Logic is an important part of all programs.

Computers can't think for themselves. They know what to do by carefully going through a set of questions that the programmer has written in the code. By answering these questions, they make the right choice.

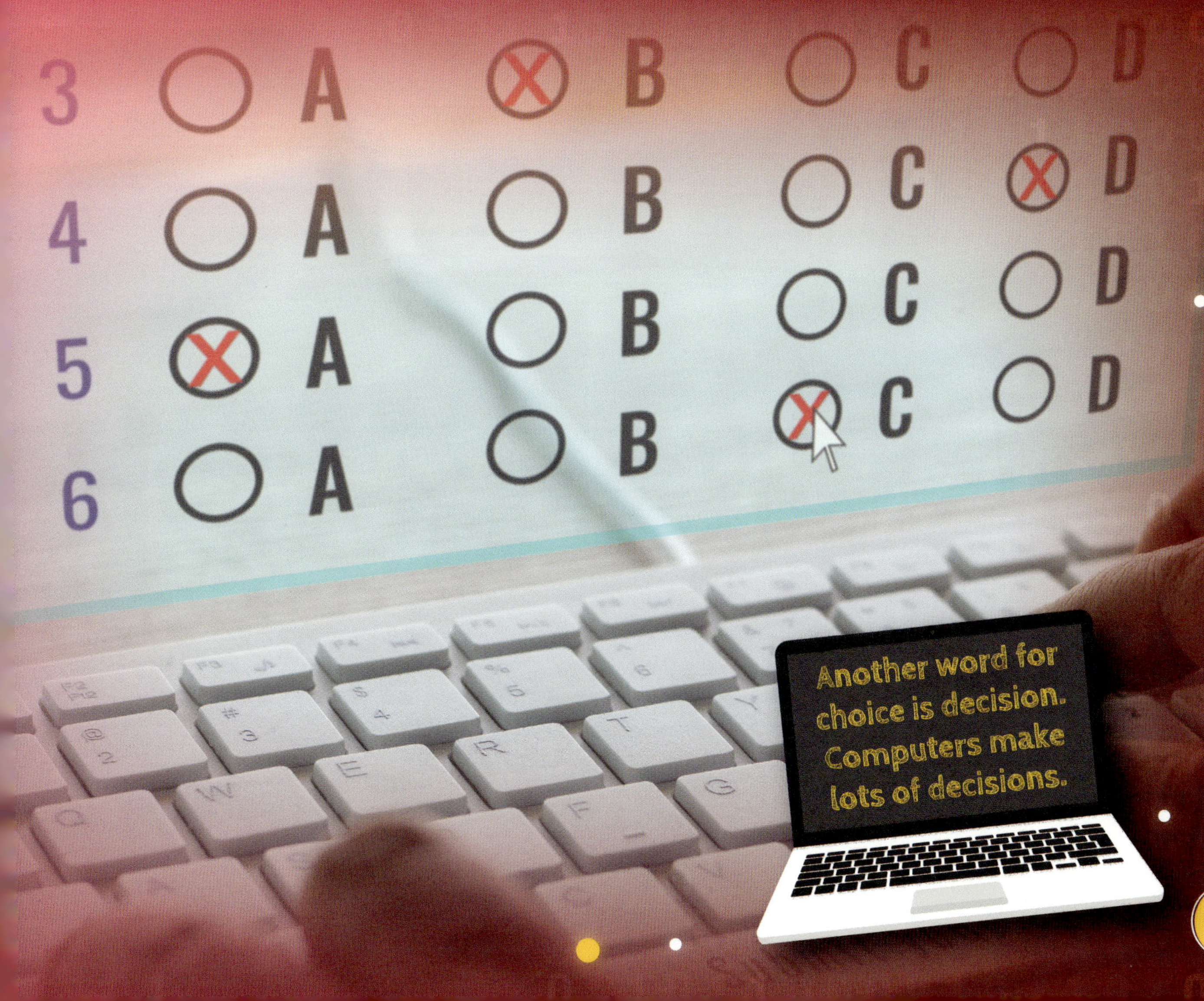

Another word for choice is decision. Computers make lots of decisions.

TRUE OR FALSE?

The most basic type of question written in code is a true or false question. The computer asks itself if something is true or false. It does different things depending on the answer.

Different answers mean the computer follows different instructions in the code.

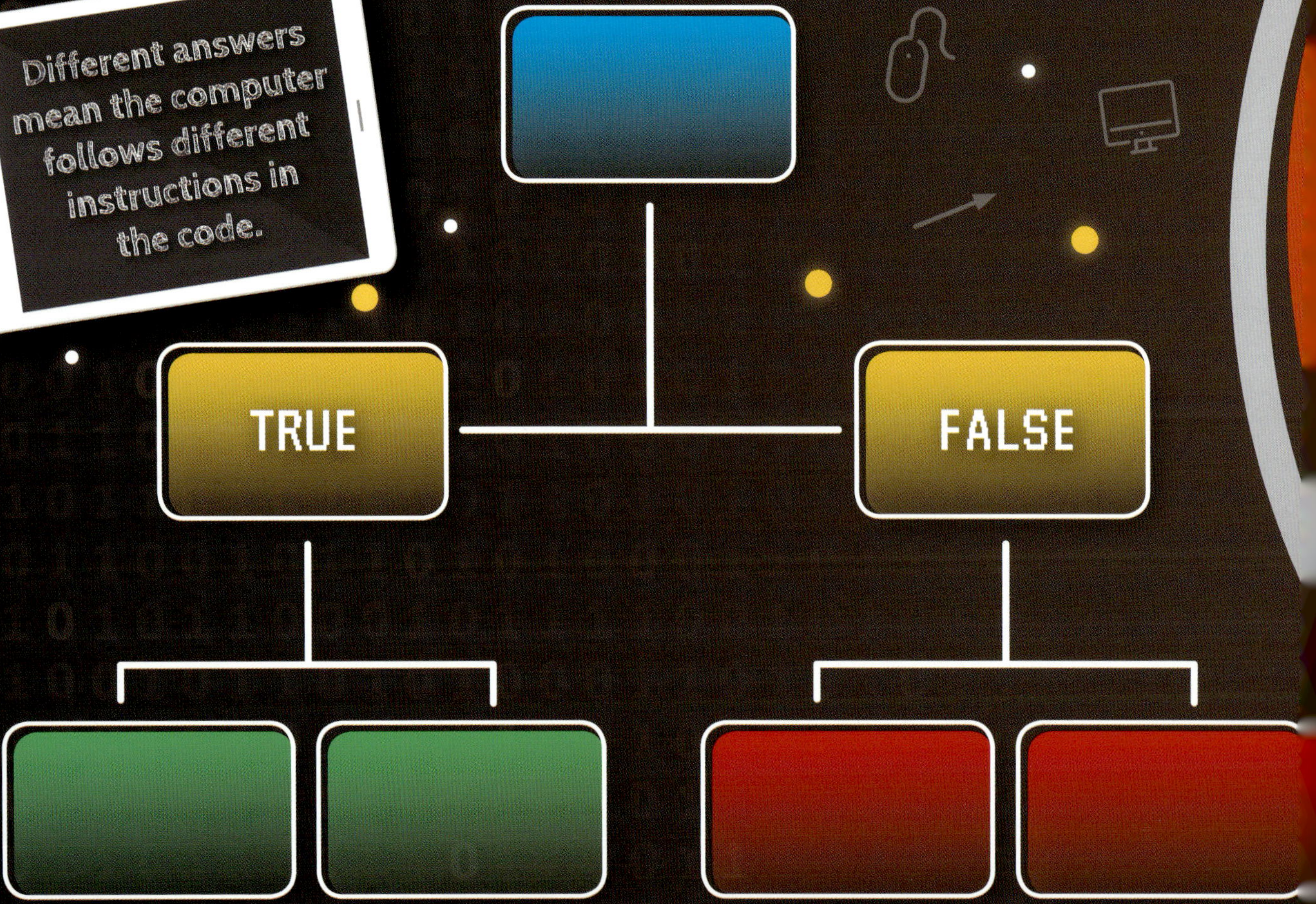

A computer will ask itself whether lots of different things are true or false. Here is an example.

The mouse has moved in the last 30 minutes. True or false?

If it is false, the computer will make itself "sleep" because nobody is using it. If it is true and someone is moving the mouse, the computer will stay on.

IF, THEN, ELSE

Coding uses conditionals to help computers decide what to do if something is true or false. There are three main parts to basic conditionals: "if," "then," and "else."

Conditionals have branches that come off them, just like the picture below. The computer follows different sets of code depending on which branch it takes.

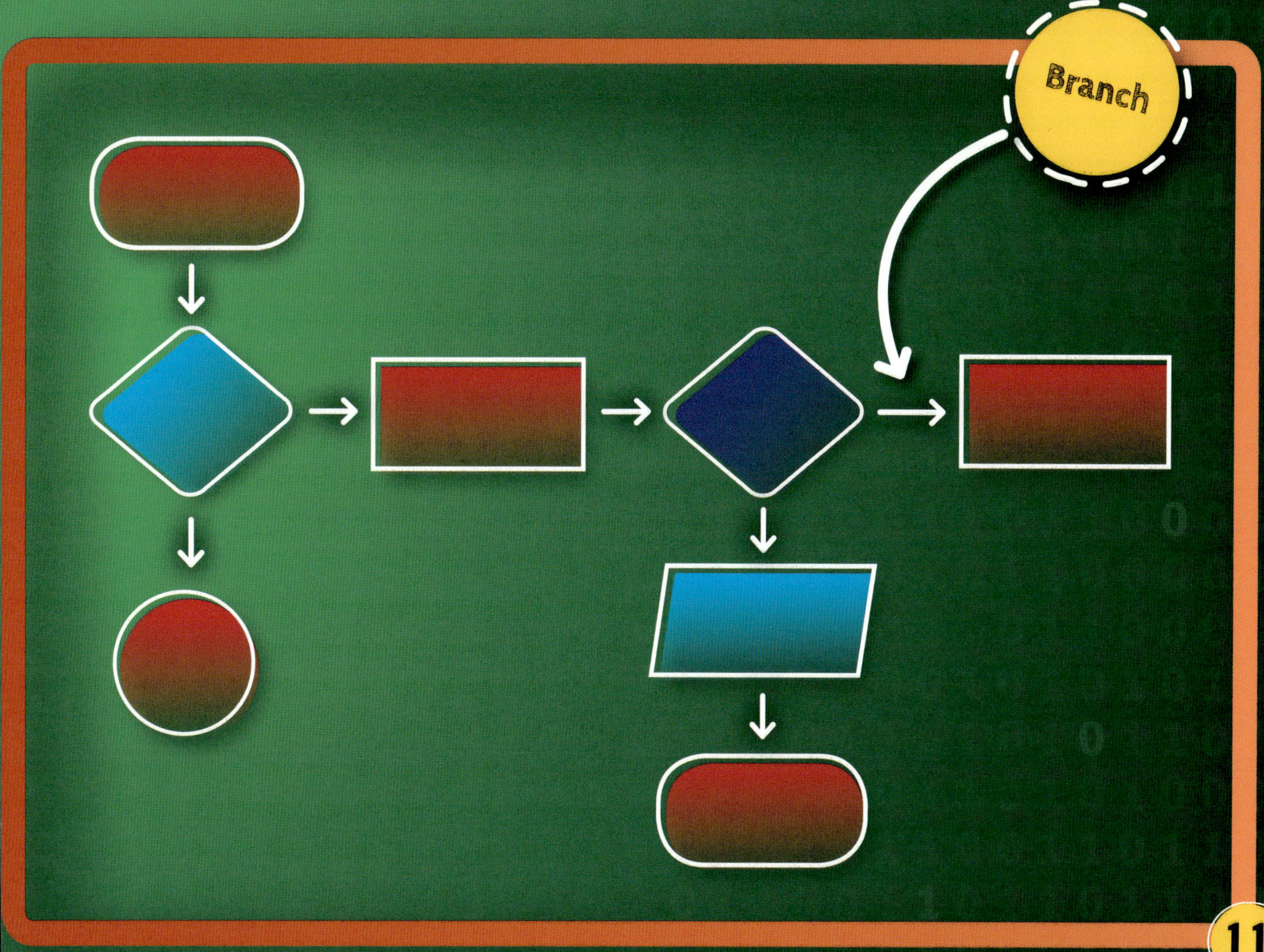

IF, THEN

The computer checks if something is true or false. If it is true, it moves down the "then" branch to the next step.

The "then" branch tells the computer what to do.

ELSE

If the conditional is false, the computer follows a different branch. It is called "else," and it tells the computer a different set of instructions.

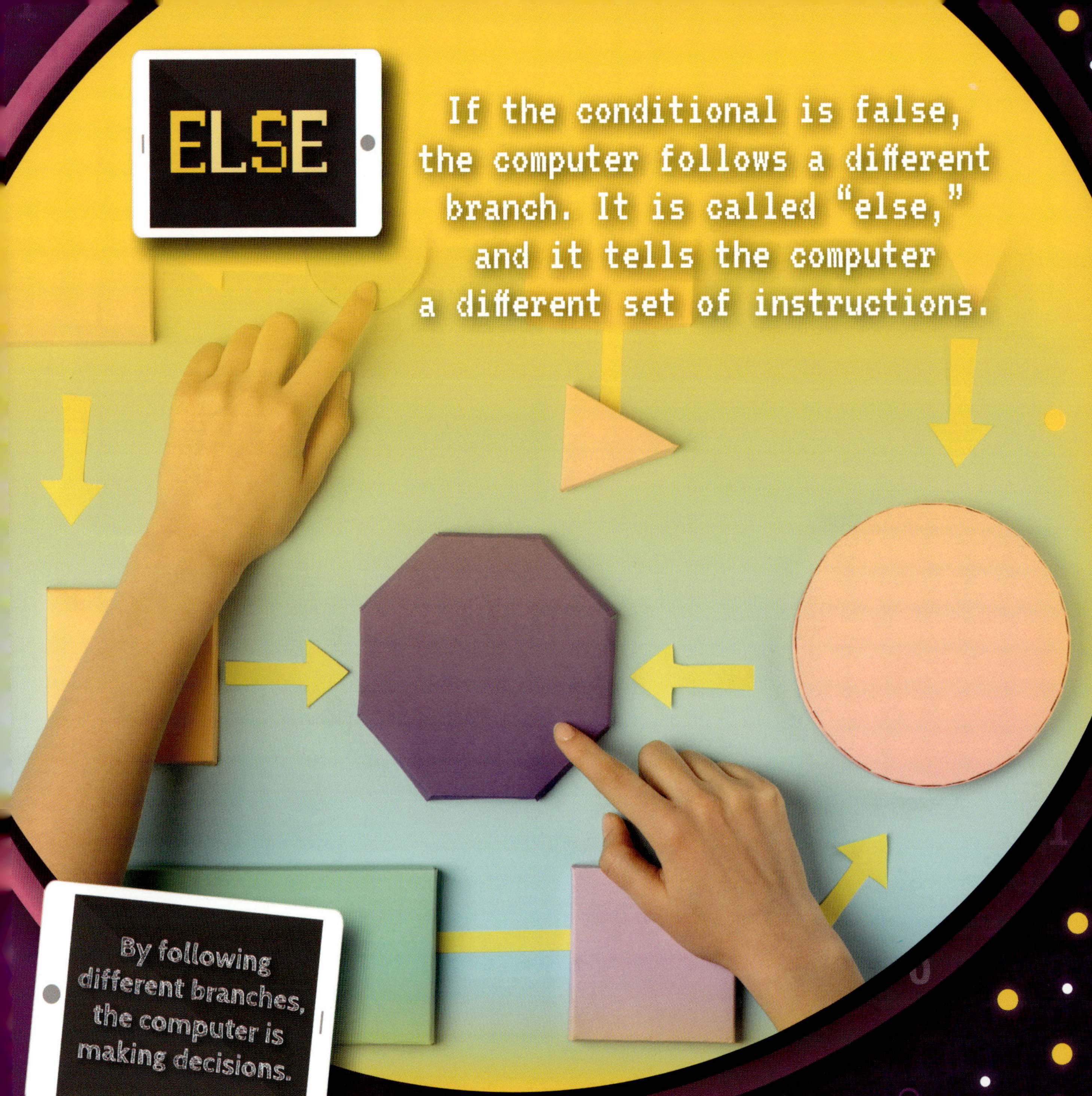

By following different branches, the computer is making decisions.

WHILE AND LOOPS

Sometimes a programmer wants a computer to do the same task over and over again. Instead of writing the same piece of code lots of times, programmers create loops.

A loop is a set of instructions that are repeated by the computer.

```
unction nextUid() {
  var index = uid.length;
  var digit;

  while(index) {
    index--;
    digit = uid[index].charCodeAt(0);
    if (digit == 57 /*'9'*/) {
      uid[index] = 'A';
      return uid.join('');
    }
    if (digit == 90  /*'Z'*/) {
      uid[index] = '0';
    } else {
      uid[index] = String.fromCharCode(digit + 1);
      return uid.join('');
    }
  }
  uid.unshift('0');
  return uid.join('');
}
```

Some programming languages create loops by using an instruction called "while." For example, the programmer will tell the computer:

WHILE stopwatch is on, keep counting up

Using "while" will keep the computer following the same instruction in a loop.

AND, OR, NOT

Programmers use logic gates to help computers make choices. Here are three very simple logic gates. In each logic gate, the computer is given two bits of information, A and B.

AND

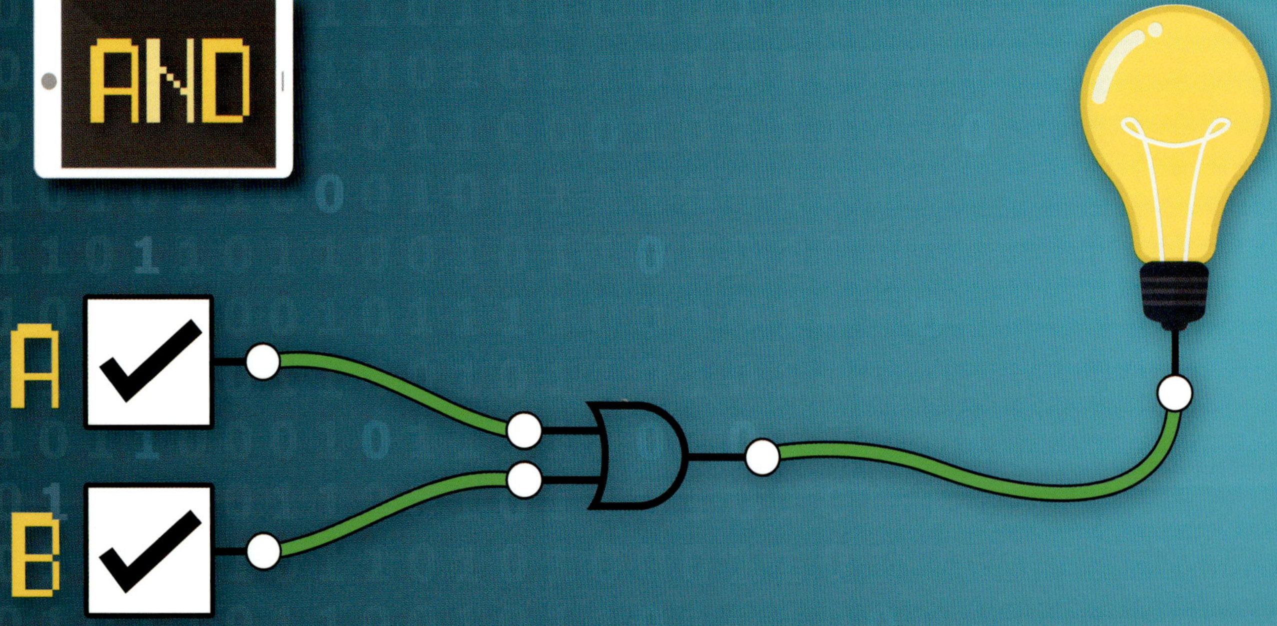

The computer follows the next instructions if both A and B are true.

The computer follows the next instructions if A is true or if B is true. It also works if both are true.

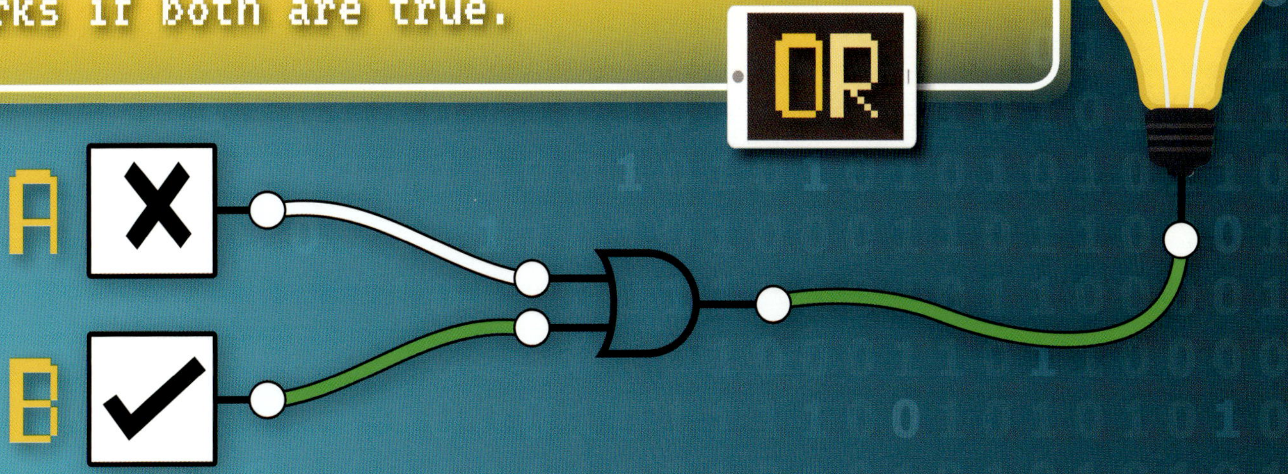

The computer follows the next instructions if A and B are false.

OTHER SYMBOLS

Lots of math symbols are used to help computers make choices. Here are a few examples.

This symbol means more than. It tells the computer to follow the next instructions if the number on the left is larger than the number on the right.

>

This symbol means less than. It tells the computer to follow the next instructions if the number on the left is smaller than the number on the right.

<

This symbol checks if two things are the same. It tells the computer to follow the next instructions if one thing is the same as another.

==

/ and *

In programming, / is used to divide numbers and * is used to multiply them together.

WHAT CAN CODING DO?

Coding can do all sorts of amazing things in the real world. For example, many programmers make video games. Some games are small and simple enough for smartphones, while others are big and complicated.

Complicated games are often played on game consoles.

Most games are made by big teams of programmers, but a programmer can make a game on their own. If you became a programmer, you could create your own video game!

FAMOUS PROGRAMMERS

AUDREY TANG

Programmer and Government Minister

Audrey Tang is an important member of the government of Taiwan. She is thought of as one of Taiwan's brightest programmers. She also set up her own company when she was 16 years old.

MARGARET HAMILTON

Computer Scientist

Margaret Hamilton was a famous computer scientist. She wrote code for the command and lunar modules used to take people to the moon for the first time. She worked on the most complicated computer system at the time.

GLOSSARY

command and lunar modules spacecraft used to go to the moon

complicated made of many different parts and therefore harder to understand

divide work out how many times one number goes into another

game consoles machines mainly used to play video games

instructions a set of steps that explain how something is done

logic gates the parts of a code that take in information and decide whether something is true or false

multiply add a number to itself a certain number of times

programming languages languages that humans use to write instructions for computers

run when a computer reads through all the instructions and does what it is told

store keep in order to use later

INDEX